PIANO · VOCAL · GUITAR

The Christian Wedding Songbook

ISBN 0-634-02169-9

HAL•LEONARD® CORPORATION

7777 W. BLUEMOUND RD. P.O. BOX 13819 MILWAUKEE, WI 53213

Visit Hal Leonard Online at
www.halleonard.com

CONTENTS

BONDED TOGETHER

Words and Music by
TWILA PARIS

Moderately, flowing

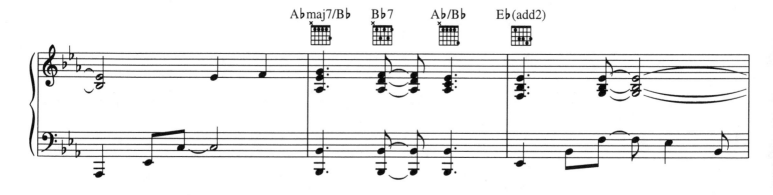

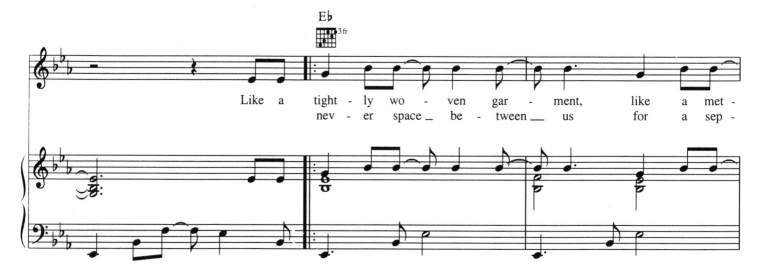

Like a tight-ly wo-ven gar-ment, like a met-
nev-er space be-tween us for a sep-

D.S. al Coda

I am cling - ing too. ____

CODA

- er. ____

I am ____ Your ser - vant ____ for - ev - er. ____

I will nev - er leave ____ You; ____

CHERISH THE TREASURE

Words and Music by
JON MOHR

BUTTERFLY KISSES

Words and Music by BOB CARLISLE
and RANDY THOMAS

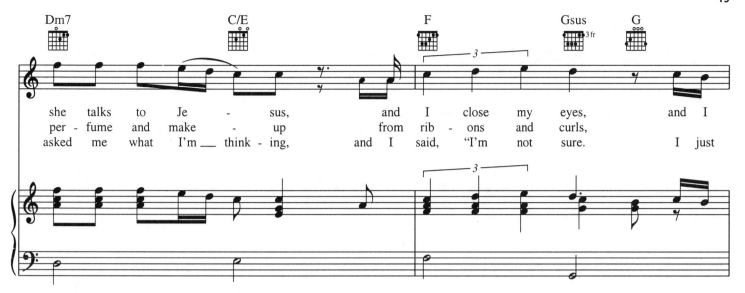

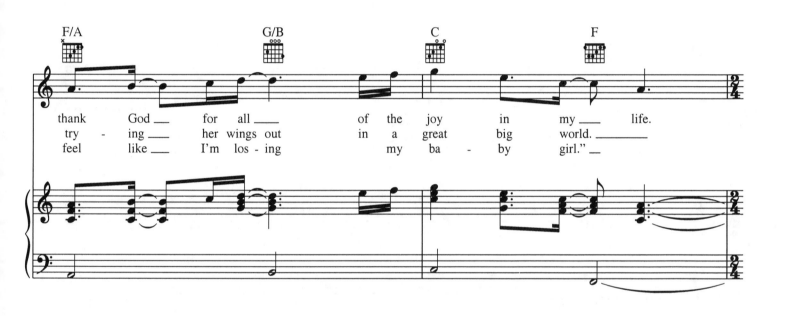

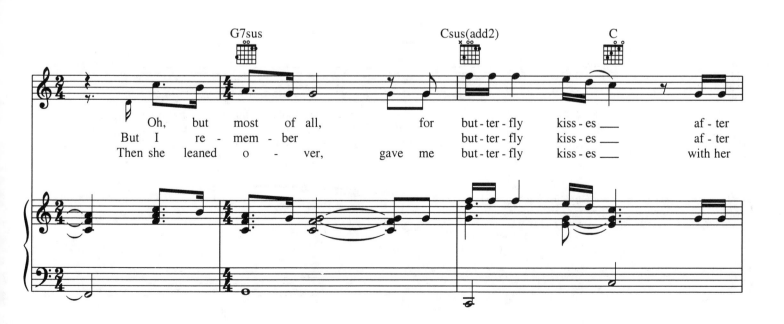

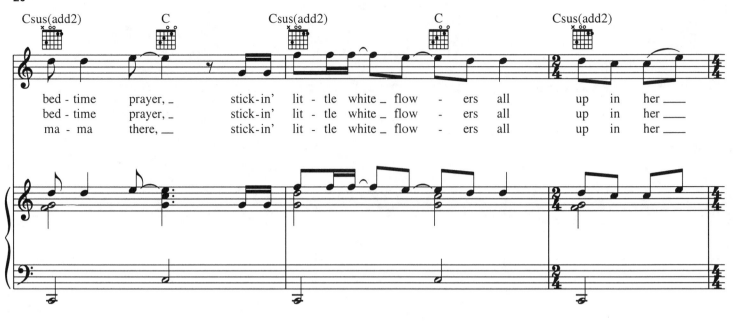

bed - time prayer, ___ stick-in' lit - tle white ___ flow - ers all up in her ___
bed - time prayer, ___ stick-in' lit - tle white ___ flow - ers all up in her ___
ma - ma there, ___ stick-in' lit - tle white ___ flow - ers all up in her ___

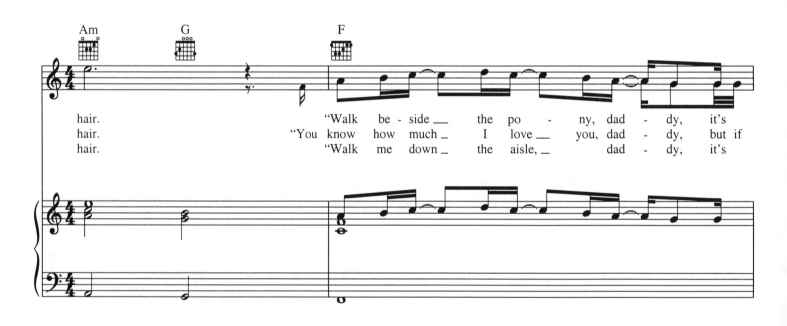

hair. "Walk be - side ___ the po - ny, dad - dy, it's
hair. "You know how much ___ I love ___ you, dad - dy, but if
hair. "Walk me down ___ the aisle, ___ dad - dy, it's

my first ride. ___ I know the cake ___ looks fun - ny, dad - dy, but
you don't mind, ___ I'm on - ly goin' to kiss ___ you on ___ the
just a - bout time. Does my wed - ding gown ___ look pret - ty, dad - dy? Dad -

COMMITMENT SONG

Words and Music by ROBERT STERLING
and CHRIS MACHEN

FAITHFUL FRIEND

Words and Music by TWILA PARIS
and STEVEN CURTIS CHAPMAN

FLESH OF MY FLESH

Words and Music by
LEON PATILLO

I do pledge my life to you,
I do give my life to you,

for - ev - er and al -
to - day and ev - 'ry __

- ways. __
__ day. __

I will take good care of you and
I will stand right by your side, what -

show - er you __ with praise. __
ev - er comes __ our way. __

GO THERE WITH YOU

Words and Music by
STEVEN CURTIS CHAPMAN

Moderately, with emotion

I know you've heard me say these
words be- fore; but ev-'ry time I say, "I love you," the

see it in your tears, you won-der where you are. The wind is grow-ing cold-er and the

HOUSEHOLD OF FAITH

Words by BRENT LAMB
Music by JOHN ROSASCO

Here we are____ at the start,____ com - mit - ting to____ each
Now to be____ a fam - i - ly____ we've got to love____ each

oth - er____ by His Word and from our hearts,
oth - er at an - y cost un - self - ish - ly;

GOD CAUSES ALL THINGS TO GROW

Words and Music by STEVEN CURTIS CHAPMAN
and STEVE GREEN

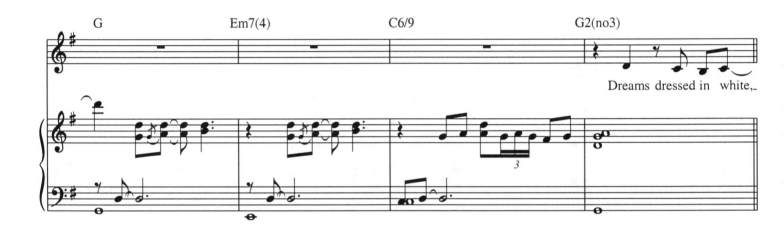

Dreams dressed in white,

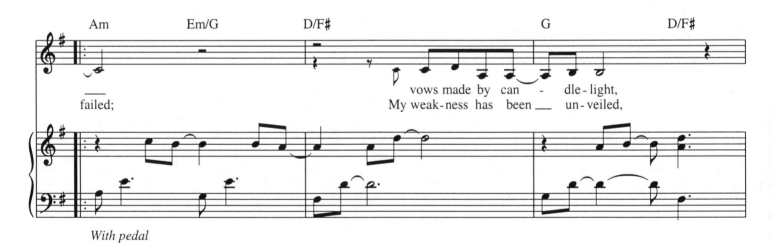

failed; vows made by can-dle-light, My weak-ness has been __ un-veiled,

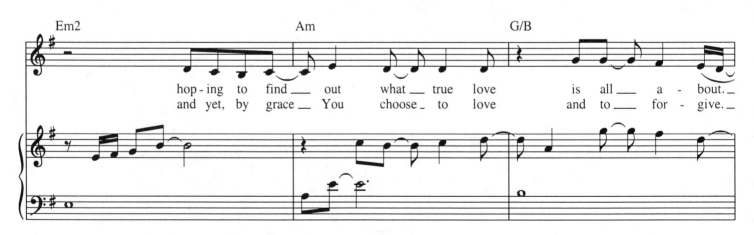

hop-ing to find __ out what __ true love is all __ a-bout.
and yet, by grace __ You choose to love and to __ for-give.

HOW BEAUTIFUL

Words and Music by
TWILA PARIS

I COULD NEVER PROMISE YOU

Moderately

Words and Music by
DON FRANCISCO

I could nev - er pro - mise you ___ on
(Verse 2: See additional lyrics)

just my **strength** a - lone. ___ That all my life I'd

care for you ___ and love you as my

Verse 2

But the love inside my heart today
  is more than mine alone;
It never changes, never fails,
  and it never seeks its own.
And by the God who gives it
  and who lives in me and you,
I know the words I speak today
  are words I'm going to do.

I.O.U. ME

Words and Music by BEBE WINANS, BILLY SPRAGUE,
KEITH THOMAS, THOMAS HEMBY and MIKE RAPP

Moderately, in 2

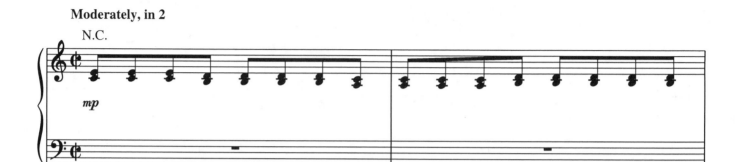

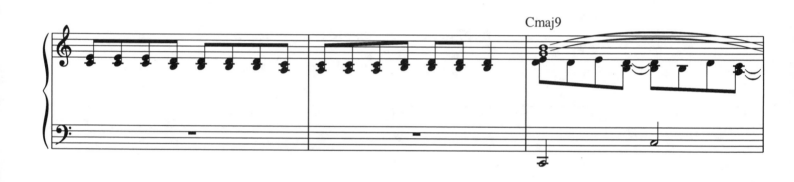

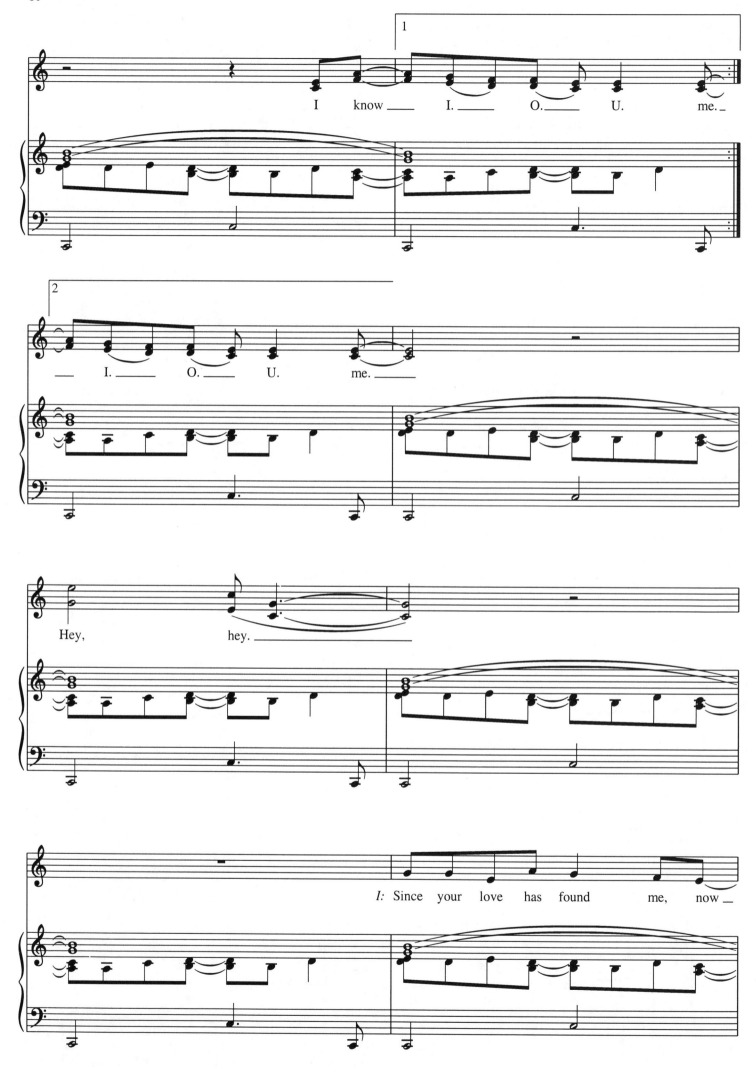

I know ___ I. ___ O. ___ U. ___ me. ___

I. ___ O. ___ U. ___ me. ___

Hey, ___ hey. ___

I: Since your love has found me, now ___

I WILL BE HERE

Words and Music by
STEVEN CURTIS CHAPMAN

IF YOU COULD SEE WHAT I SEE

Words and Music by GEOFF MOORE
and STEVEN CURTIS CHAPMAN

IN THIS VERY ROOM

Words and Music by
RON and CAROL HARRIS

THE LANGUAGE OF JESUS IS LOVE

Words and Music by PHILL McHUGH, GREG NELSON,
SCOTT WESLEY BROWN and PHIL NAISH

The lan-guage of Je-sus is love. Just one word can bring heal-ing and light to each heart that has hun-gered for kind-ness and truth through the trials and the tri-umphs of life. The

THE LORD'S PRAYER

By ALBERT HAY MALOTTE

LOST WITHOUT YOU

Words and Music by BEBE WINANS
and KEITH THOMAS

LOVE

Words and Music by
BOB HARTMAN

With feeling

Love is pa-
Love is gen-

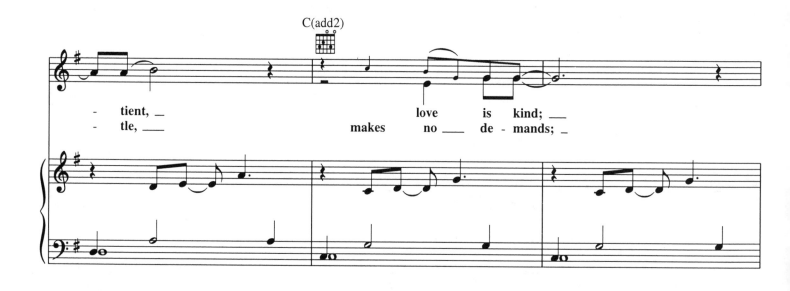

-tient, __ love is kind; __
-tle, __ makes no __ de-mands; __

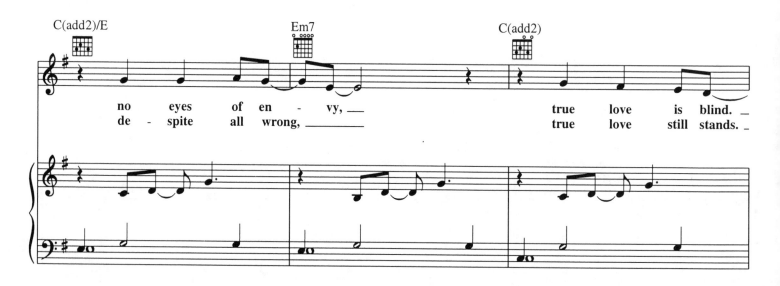

no eyes of en-vy, __ true love is blind. __
de-spite all wrong, __ true love still stands. __

sent in His Son; ___

love for - gives ___ all ___

we have ___ done.

D.S. al Coda

CODA

Love has ___ come. ___

LOVE OF THE LASTING KIND

Words and Music by CLAIRE CLONINGER
and DON CASON

LOVE THAT WILL NOT LET ME GO

Words and Music by STEVE CAMP
and ROB FRAZIER

Rubato

will not ___ let _____ me go. _____

LOVE WILL BE OUR HOME

Words and Music by
STEVEN CURTIS CHAPMAN

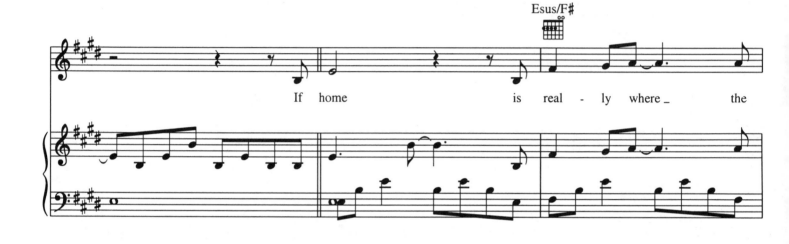

If home is real-ly where the

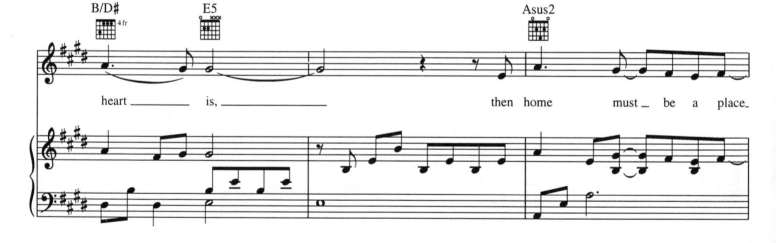

heart _____ is, _____ then home must_ be a place_

___ we all can ____ share. _____ For

MAKE US ONE

Words and Music by
PAUL JOHNSON

O HOW HE LOVES YOU AND ME

Words and Music by
KURT KAISER

O how He loves you and me! O how He loves you and me! He gave His life, what more could He give?

ONLY GOD COULD LOVE YOU MORE

Words and Music by DWIGHT LILES
and NILES BOROP

PANIS ANGELICUS
(O Lord Most Holy)

By CÉSAR FRANCK

ra - bi-lis, man - du - cat Do - mi-num Pau - per, _

O res mi - ra - bi-lis, man - du - cat Do - mi-num

ff

pau - per, ser - vus et hu - mi - lis, Pau - per, _

ff

Pau - per, _ ser - vus et hu - mi - lis, Pau - per, _

I,II unison

pau - per, ser - vus, _ ser - vus et hu - mi - lis.

decresc.

p

PARENT'S PRAYER
(Let Go of Two)

Words and Music by
GREG DAVIS

With feeling

I guess we have al - ways known _ that a
Now in your ten - der care, _ Lord, _

day like this _ one would come, _ when our chil - dren would leave _
be all that we _ can - not be. _ And help us to trust _

— us and be - gin to build a home of their own. _
— You when we don't see You quick - ly meet - ing their needs. _

SHINE ON US

Words and Music by MICHAEL W. SMITH
and DEBBIE SMITH

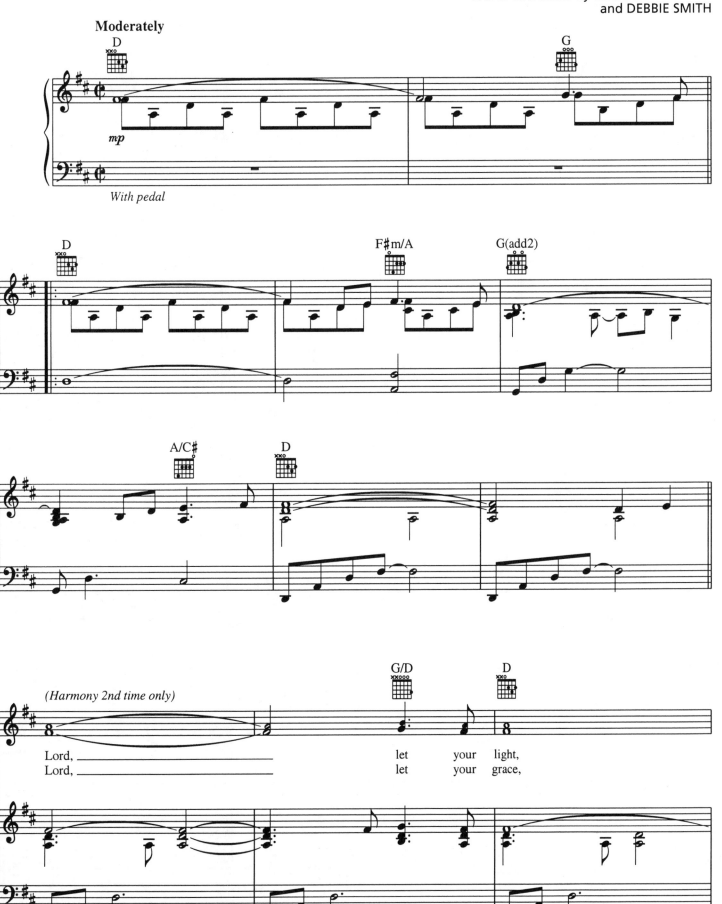

PERFECT UNION

Words and Music by JOHN ANDREW SCHREINER
and MATTHEW WARD

Steady four

There's a love __ that lasts __ a life-
And there are times __ in ev-'ry un-
Hand in hand __ we seek __ the Fa-

-time,
-ion
-ther

love be-tween __ a man __ and
when hard times __ and trou-ble
and the Fa-ther's pre-cious

wife. _____
fall, _____
Son, _____

Love so strong __ it goes __ be-yond __ our rea- son.
tear-ing at __ the seams __ of __ love, _____
and the pow-er of __ His __ Spir- it

PORTRAIT OF LOVE

Words and Music by KENNY WOOD
and BILLY CROCKETT

SEEKERS OF YOUR HEART

Words and Music by MELODIE TUNNEY,
DICK TUNNEY and BEVERLY DARNALL

THIS IS THE DAY
(A Wedding Song)

Words and Music by
SCOTT WESLEY BROWN

THIS VERY DAY

Words and Music by JOHN ELLIOTT
and PAUL OVERSTREET

I've been search-ing all __ my life __ for the wom-an I __ was meant __ to make __ my __ wife. And

Like the an-swer to __ my prayers, __ from this day on __ I'll wake __ to find __ her __ there. And

WEDDING PRAYER

By FERN G. DUNLAP

Reverently

Heav - en - ly Fa - ther, hear us as we pray,

Here at Thine al - tar, on our wed - ding day.

Show us the path that Thou would'st have us take;

TIME FOR JOY

Words and Music by
GERRY LIMPIC

THE WEDDING

Words and Music by
MICHAEL CARD

Lord ___ of light, oh come to this wed-ding; _ take ___ the doubt and dark-ness a-way. Turn ___ the wa-ter of life-less liv-ing ___

WEDDING PRAYER

Words and Music by
MARY RICE HOPKINS